Printed in Great Britain
by Amazon

12897662R00059